The Musician's Guide To
Music Publishing
In The UK

Paul Baxter

Published by the Author
2014

Typesetting: Adobe Garamond 12pt

TABLE OF CONTENTS

List Of Figures

Chapter 1: What Is Music Publishing?

1.1. Intellectual Property

Firstly, music publishing and publishing are two entirely different things. Publishing usually refers to the release of material in forms such as magazines, websites, novels etc. Music publishing, however, refers to a group of rights, specifically for the intellectual property of music and lyrics. It is the exploitation and collection of royalties, for these rights.

The term 'intellectual property', comes from the fact that in the UK, the copyright of a piece of music comes into being, at the point when the creator thinks it up. There is often a lot of misunderstanding surrounding copyrighting material. Often, the recommendation is bounced around, that a recording or sheet music should be posted to yourself by recorded delivery, and not opened until required legally and that this creates the copyright on your material. This is also often countered by people who say that this is not enough to copyright a work, or means nothing, leaving the musician in a state of confusion and panic over the safety of their hard work.

In fact, what is required in the UK, is PROOF that the music was thought up by you, rather than by someone else. Posting it recorded delivery to yourself could be extremely handy in proving that you had the idea before someone else, but it's worth bearing in mind, for example, that if you have written music for a group and post yourself a recording of them playing your song and it's that same group who you are in a dispute with, that crafty proof may be worth very little.

In fact, it is also worth registering works with the US Copyright Office if you are serious and believe your music may be used at a later date, across the pond. This can be a costly procedure, especially if you write twenty songs about twenty objects in your room every day. It does put you in an excellent position legally though, if ever challenged.

In the US, copyright exists when the work is recorded into a tangible form of media, from which it can be reproduced. A legal challenge of copyright infringement can't be entered into through a federal court over there, unless a work is first registered with the US Copyright Office. This registration can be used as proof in Europe.

Therefore, for a cost-effective method until things start to take off, you could reduce your costs and use the postage method. Just remember to get it sent by RECORDED delivery, so that the post office stamp the date of postage, otherwise you may be left with little more than a waste of a CD and your time.

Be wary of companies offering to copyright your material, as they will unlikely be able to provide much more than a recorded delivery package would.

1.2. Music Publishing Rights Vs. Master/Sound Rights

One of the biggest areas of confusion is in the difference between publishing rights and master (sound) rights. The master rights are the copyrights linked with a specific recording of a work. The copyright owners in this case would be the record label and the artists performing on the recording. Remember, that music publishing refers to the actual song, not any particular recording of a song or artist performing it.

MASTER RIGHTS → copyrights linked with a specific recording of a work (owner is label or artist performing the song)

So to help you to understand this concept, see figure 1 below showing two recordings of the same song:

```
A - Girl I love you
Written by: Patti Gerald
Artist: Smooth DJ
        Tiger Records
```

```
B - Girl I love you
Written by: Patti Gerald
Artist: Michelle Waite
        Lonely Recordings
```

Figure 1.

Whenever recording A is used, Patti Gerald will receive publishing royalties for writing the song, and Smooth DJ/Tiger Records will receive royalties for the master rights.

Whenever recording B is used, Patti Gerald will again receive publishing royalties for writing the song, and Michelle Waite/Lonely Recordings will this time receive royalties for the master rights. Anyone wishing to use a recording to promote a product, etc, will need to clear (gain a license to use, and negotiate a fee for that usage) both rights separately with their rights holders or those who represent them. This book discusses the issues concerning publishing rights.

MUSIC CLEARANCE : every commercial track has 2 components to clear
- recording (lyrics + notes recorded, owned + administered by record label)
- publishing (lyrics + notes, owned by publisher or rightsholder)

TO CLEAR PUBLISHING → PRS for Music offers license agreement (IPC Scheme) which you can use to license tracks → locate track with the "work search" function on the PRS database and ensure all the final owners are 100% MCPS + PRS registered

8

Chapter 2: A Breakdown Of Right Types

Music publishing refers to a group of rights, each of those rights refers to a way in which your copyright as a songwriter is used. For each type of right, different companies or processes are used in order to grant permission for use (licenses) and collect royalties for that use. Let's break them down and take a look at who would use them:

Performing right – this is the most common right that a less established performer may rely on for some extra money. The performing right is wherever somebody can hear your music, be it at a live event, over the radio, on the television or over the internet. A not-for-profit organisation in the UK, called PRS or the Performing Rights Society, licenses these companies and collects royalties on your behalf.

Mechanical right – this is where a song or musical work is transferred from one device to another, without the music necessarily being heard. Examples of this include writing music onto a CD, transferring it from a PC to an iPod, downloading a track from iTunes onto your PC, etc.

this means that the publisher is allowing PRS to license the track and collect royalties for the publishing on their behalf

TO CLEAR RECORDINGS → locate the track on CPL Audio repertoire search and check that the recording is owned by a CPL registered record label

9

In the times of cassettes, a new payment of royalties was paid per cassette, called the 'blank tape levy'. This was because so many people recorded music onto these blank cassettes, that a royalty was paid mostly to the artists and songwriters of the biggest works at the time, with the assumption that it would be their music that was being copied.

Where music usage required a mechanical and a performance license (such as in the online world), people and companies wishing to use music would have had to go to both PRS and MCPS to obtain two separate licenses (as well as clear the Master rights separately). To make this process easier, PRS and MCPS joined forces in 1997 as the MCPS-PRS Alliance and were rebranded again a few years ago as PRS For Music. The larger branding contains the two companies, PRS and MCPS, who can offer 'joint licenses'. They shares most departments, buildings and were seen as one company. More recently, PRS bought out MCPS' shares.

The synch right (or synchronisation right) – some musicians write music specifically for adverts, movies and television. Although they will be paid a performance and mechanical royalty, every time the usage is aired on TV or pressed/sold on DVD, they will also be paid a synch royalty (we will look at more in-depth structures later in the book). A synch right is where a piece of music is put to image. The production company making the advert, film or television show, must first seek permission from the rights holder to use the music. Once agreed, a one-off payment will usually be negotiated. If the deal changes to include new territories or run for longer, another fee will be paid. Some songwriters deny usage which come into conflict with their set-out 'moral rights' (this is a term referring to your rights as a musician and is not a publishing 'right', so don't be confused). 'Moral rights' are where a songwriter may refuse to allow a company to use their music, if they don't agree with their morals. It could be a fast food chain, a political party, a company with a bad reputation, pornography or just a project that they feel could harm their own image or their relationship with their fans, the press and/or the general public.

Print right – A common example of print rights is in guitar tablature books, piano books or lyrics on websites. It is where the lyrics and/or the non-audio form of the music is made available. This is dealt with the musician directly.

Other – There are a couple of areas not included in the above (such as 'grand rights' for musicals, often dealt with by the writer or their publisher directly, as will be discussed later, as well as karaoke, ringtones, etc.). However, these are not mainstream and for the sake of keeping this book as simple as possible, we'll just concentrate on the four rights as described above.

LICENSEE —> one who holds (or wants to hold) a piece of music by
LICENSOR —> obtaining a license

Chapter 3: The Basic Structure Of The UK Music Publishing Sector

3.1. Direct Licensing

The structure of the UK music publishing sector can get quite complicated, so let's start small. <u>A songwriter holds all the rights and the licensees want to use that music.</u> A licensee is someone who holds (or in this instance, wants to hold) a license to use a piece of music.

Figure 2 represets the movement of publishing rights in its simplest form, from the songwriter to the people who wish to use their music. Now, as straightforward as this looks, if we split up the licensees into a more realistic form, as shown in figure 3, we can see that for someone who wants to write and, usually, also perform their music, this seems a little more daunting.

Now, if this doesn't seem like much then try to break down each box. Record labels are probably the least daunting but think of issuing a license every time your song is released on a compilation album, assuming you have a big hit. That's doable, but now think of the next category. If you were to write a hit and everyone wanted to hear it,

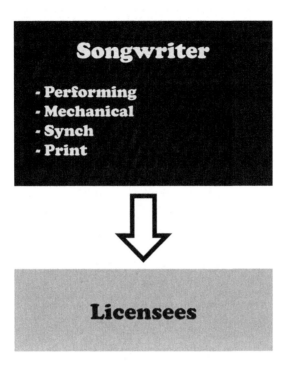

Figure 2.

could you issue a license to every hairdresser, pub, bowling alley, cinema, restaurant, retail outlet, coffee shop and nightclub that wanted to use it? On the other hand, could a single one of those businesses ever find the time to obtain a license for the use of every song they play? That, in itself, would be a full-time job.

This is where collection societies come onto the scene. Without collection societies, the music publishing industry would not be able to cope. There would be no way of monitoring or collecting information about music usage on a large scale. A collection society will obtain permission from the writer to further license the usage to others, and will collect the royalties for that usage, passing it back to the rights holder, taking a commission. The commission varies over different usage types. For current commission rates, check the PRS For Music website or phone in to ask directly.

COLLECTION SOCIETY
↓
will obtain permission from the writer to further license the usage to others and will collect the royalties on behalf of the rights holder

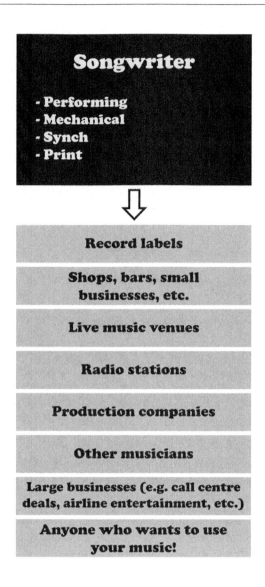

Figure 3.

3.2. Adding A Collection Society

There are two rights that a collection society deals with, performing and mechanical rights. This is because these are the two that are most

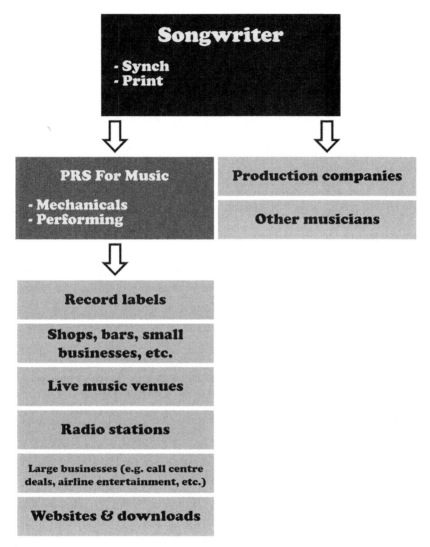

Figure 4.

used to a less-controllable degree within the territory (as discussed previously, with the shops, restaurants, websites, etc.).

In most territories outside of the UK, one company administers the performing right and another the mechanical (or one company administers both, like in the UK). In the US, there are two main (ASCAP and BMI) and one smaller (SESAC) performing societies competing within the same territory. However, this is unusual.

Figure 4, above, shows us that some of the burden has been taken from the writer and processed by these societies for a fee. Some societies worldwide are privately owned and work for a profit, but PRS For Music in the UK is a not-for-profit entity.

Keep in mind that as with every other area in the music industry (agents, management, etc.) or any other services in life (cleaners, PAs, etc.), the more you do yourself, the larger percentage of the original amount you get, but also the more work you will have to do.

Chapter 4: PRS For Music

4.1. Reporting & Licenses

PRS For Music is, as expected, a very large company of around 800 employees, multiple offices and regional staff. It deals with thousands of companies across the UK, and works with other societies internationally (as we'll discuss, in a little more depth, later).

As mentioned earlier, it would be impossible for anyone, even an organisation as large as PRS For Music, to issue a license for every music usage in the UK. To evade this problem, PRS issue many companies with a 'blanket license'. A blanket license is where the company pays a set, annual fee for the use of any song. This brings the number of required licenses for a company from thousands per year, to just one.

The downside to this is accuracy. A few companies that pay annual, blanket licenses, provide accurate data for most of their usage. This includes the BBC, who provide PRS with details of songs played across their radio stations, for example. The vast majority of small businesses, however, are subject to sampling, whereby whatever is played during a set time period is paid (could be as small as one day a year) and many users aren't sampled, but their license fees are paid out to the songs which had the highest radio play, elsewhere.

It's unfair to hold the businesses accountable. Many, such as hairdressers and retail outlets, just pay a license to play the radio to customers, in an attempt to create a desired, relaxed atmosphere. It's also unfair to hold PRS For Music accountable, as to increase accuracy to anywhere close to 100%, would cost far more than the sector brings in, resulting in songwriters earning nothing.

New technology, known as 'fingerprint technology', is starting to emerge. Codes broadcast within a piece of music, allow devices to pick up what is being played and when. This could increase accuracy in radio broadcasts multiple times over, but will still unlikely cover every music usage all over the UK.

The birth of digital has brought with it, both blessings and challenges. iTunes allows tracking for every download, so that royalties can be split specifically between works. On the other end of the spectrum, Youtube is a giant melting pot of user-generated content. From official music videos, released by the record labels, to amusing parodies of dancing cats, dressed as elves, music is widely used. Although Youtube pay an annual blanket license to PRS For Music (so uploaders don't have to gain a license or pay a fee – it's paid for through advertising profits), matching of this music usage, especially on videos that receive low 'hits', becomes something of a challenge.

The department that deals with licenses for physical products have an account management system in place. Every so often they monitor new releases by their accounts.

For television, 'cue sheets' (a list of all works used in a program or film) are gathered and matched to works on the database. Then information is gathered from each channel, on which films, programs and adverts were shown, and linked to cue sheets.

It gets even more complicated, where multiple licenses are required. A sitcom, for example, will require a synch license from the rights holder, in order to put music to image. Then the television channel will require a blanket license in order to air the program. Finally, whoever releases the sitcom on DVD, will require a mechanical license to press them. Any website showing on-demand or catchup streams, will require a further license to do so as well.

Another example would be a hairdresser's salon, that plays its radio for customers to listen to while they have their hair styled (or butchered, if the music is especially gripping). The radio station pay a license fee in order to broadcast music and the salon will require a public performance license in order to further use this music to create a required atmosphere for its business.

4.2. Getting Paid To Play

One area, which would be of the most interest to less established musicians who gig regularly, is that of the live performance. In the UK, there is a rare situation, where almost any live performance is paid. In places such as the US, only the top gigs and tours per year are paid out on, including fees brought in from smaller gigs.

In the UK, however, PRS For Music just need to know details of the gig and obtain a setlist, in order to pay out. For gigs played in a live music venue, the publishing royalty is usually around 3% of the box-office takings, split equally between all the songs of the show, by all bands. This is worth keeping in mind, if you ever find yourself supporting a major act at Wembley. The promoter might pay you £200 and throw a couple of sandwiches and cans of beer your way, but the PRS For Music royalties could be in the thousands.

The PRS Gigs & Clubs scheme is fairly new, by only a matter of a few years. This covers smaller shows, played in small clubs, pubs and unusual locations (such as under a bridge or a warehouse). As long as a license fee has been paid by a location. You won't get paid for example, just for randomly setting up a show in Samantha's basement, as where would the money come from to pay you? Not unless Samantha's mum has a live music license.

In a perfect world, the concert promoter or venue will submit a setlist to PRS For Music, who will match up the songs on their database and pay out. This is normal for very large promoters, who strike up relationships with their acts, offering it as an added service, and who know a bit about publishing royalties. It's unlikely, however, that your mate's uncle, who fancies his hand at putting on a gig, will know anything about it. There's a section on the PRS For Music website (once you join and receive log in details), where you can submit your setlist. It's worth doing this, just to be sure.

The PRS Gigs & Clubs scheme, as it accounts for smaller venues, which will have far lower yearly license fees, won't pay out a lot. It could add up to around £2-£5 per night. It doesn't seem as much but the earning can potentially add up to a larger sum. I once encountered a folk musician, who traveled around Scotland, and played around 250-300 gigs in the past year. He submitted his setlists after having been informed of this scheme, and ended up with about a £1000 that he wasn't even expecting. Every little helps, especially for someone who relies on performing their own music as their main source of income.

Please note though, that for every cover that you play, the royalties for that song will go to the writers and not to you for performing it. On the flip side, if someone covers your song, then (providing PRS For Music are made aware and the venue/radio station, etc., is licensed) you will be paid publishing royalties and not them for performing it.

4.3. Understanding Where The Money Comes From

If you believe that you are entitled to money then the thing that should be thought about first is where that money would come from. One scenario, which crops up often in the music publishing sector, is where a musician makes a few hundred copies of their album to sell at gigs. They then get in contact with PRS For Music or their publisher and demand missing royalties. The only income from sales of the CD would be from the purchaser at the gig, so who would be paying them these missing royalties?

For CDs, the record label pays publishing royalties based on either

4. PRS For Music

the number of units that were pressed (for smaller labels and releases), or on what has left the warehouse, with allowance for breakage and returns (for the major record labels and releases). Therefore, if you make a few hundred copies of an album, then you are acting as the record label. All that PRS For Music could do is to charge you as a record label and pay you as a writer, whilst taking a commission for the transaction.

If another party releases your material, such as a record label, then you should ensure royalties are received. Even if you release your own product, and another party releases a compilation album with your track on it, then they should pay a mechanical fee for using your song.

Another area where royalties would be due to you are streaming or online downloads. As it's the website that pays a license fee, you would be entitled to royalties. Please bear in mind though, that websites such as Youtube may pay a large, annual license fee but have millions of 'hits' per day. The actual amounts earned from each 'hit' would be fractions of a penny. If you put in a lot of effort to track down royalties for a couple of hundred Youtube hits, you'll end up irritating some people. Most societies have a cut-off for Youtube, attempting to match usage on videos over a few thousand 'hits', only.

4.4. Joining And Registering Your Works

In order to obtain any royalties from PRS For Music you need to do two things. You need to join and you need to register your works with them. When you join any society, you are given a number known as an IPI number (Interested Parties Information Number). This is then your unique identifying number for your current society, or any others than you may wish to join at a later date, for different territories.

At the time of writing this, the fee for joining as a writer for the performing side (the part that used to be PRS) was £50. It's an administrative fee and results in lifetime membership. You may not be earning much (yet) from publishing royalties, but as this is a fee you would be paying at some point anyway, and you have deadlines to make claims for historic usage, it could be worth joining now.

Making claims for historic usage is called making a 'backclaim'. On the performance side, you can only backclaim up until your effective date of membership. There are two dates per year of membership, 1 January and 1 July. Even if you join on the day before the next membership date, you can backclaim to the previous effective date of membership, but not before. For example, on 30 June 2014, you could backclaim until 1 January 2014, but on 1 July 2014, you couldn't backclaim past 1 July 2014.

If you're unclear on this, or if you want to see if anything has changed since the writing of this book, it'd be worth checking out the PRS For Music website at www.prsformusic.com or speak to them directly by giving one of their advisers a call.

If you wish to join for mechanical rights, the current fee at the time of writing this, is also £50 for a writer. On the mechanical side, you can backclaim physical products in the UK for up to 6 years after release (even prior to joining date). Digital royalties, however, can't be backclaimed. So if your works are being downloaded by fans on iTunes, for example, then it may be worth joining MCPS.

Please note that these memberships are individual, so if there are four writers in your band, all four of you would need to join separately. Only a music publisher can claim royalties on behalf of someone else (as we'll come to that soon).

The second point of ensuring that your works are registered, is also vital. We will look into the whole registration process and common work splits later on, but for now it's crucial to point out that if PRS For Music don't know your work exists, then they won't know that's what's been used by a licensee and you could permanently miss out on a particular royalty. Letting them know your works exist as soon as possible can only help in ensuring that you are paid for the use of your music.

Even if a work has just been written and you haven't done anything with it yet, there's no harm in registering it with PRS For Music anyway. You may find yourself playing it live at your next gig and wanting to submit the setlist.

Often, if there is usage and PRS For Music think they may know who it belongs to, they pay it out as they believe it should be paid out. This can be very helpful in many circumstances but can also cause problems. Chances are that you would not want your royalties accidentally paid to someone else with a similar name or split out incorrectly amongst your co-writers, resulting in an uncomfortable discussion with PRS For Music about obtaining the money back from your friend to pay to you.

Chapter 5: How Is A Work Split?

This is one of the trickiest parts to explain if you are not at all familiar with music publishing. A work is made up of 200%. To be more accurate, it's made up of two sets of 100%. There is the full works split for the performing right and the full works split for the mechanical right (remember that PRS For Music deal with two kinds of rights). Usually, they're both the same, and it's just a matter of splitting the work between the writers:

Writer	IPI Number	Performance	Mechanical
Heidle, Luke	10101024	50.00%	50.00%
Clarke, Lucy	20203048	50.00%	50.00%

The actual, collective publishing rights for a work are split 50/50 between the top line melody of a work and the lyrics. So it would be normal to see what is represented in the table below, where 'C' stands for 'Composer' and 'A' denotes 'Author':

Writer	Role	IPI Number	Performance	Mechanical
Heidle, Luke	C	10101024	50.00%	50.00%
Clarke, Lucy	A	20203048	50.00%	50.00%

It is also usual to see situations where roles are mixed, such as the two examples below:

Writer	Role	IPI Number	Performance	Mechanical
Heidle, Luke	CA	10101024	50.00%	50.00%
Clarke, Lucy	CA	20203048	50.00%	50.00%

Writer	Role	IPI Number	Performance	Mechanical
Heidle, Luke	CA	10101024	75.00%	75.00%
Clarke, Lucy	C	20203048	25.00%	25.00%

These are only guidelines and while I would recommend you stick to them for simplicity's sake, you don't have to and can work it out amongst yourselves. For example, the below splits on a work written by four people, would be perfectly acceptable:

Writer	Role	IPI Number	Performance	Mechanical
Heidle, Luke	CA	10101024	33.33%	16.67%
Clarke, Lucy	CA	20203048	16.67%	33.33%
Smythe, Pete	CA	98356281	12.50%	5%
Allison, Katie	C	29463825	37.50%	45%

Just as long as both the mechanical and performance sides add up to 100% each. The two areas that you may encounter problems with are:

Writer	Role	IPI Number	Performance	Mechanical
Heidle, Luke	A	10101024	50.00%	50.00%
Clarke, Lucy	A	20203048	50.00%	50.00%

As this is a music collection society and music publishing rights, a work can't exist without a musical element. The above could only represent a poem or piece of literature and wouldn't be relevant.

Writer	Role	IPI Number	Performance	Mechanical
Heidle, Luke	C	10101024	33.33%	33.33%
Clarke, Lucy	A	20203048	33.33%	33.33%

In the above example, shares don't add up to 100% on the performance or mechanical side. It would suggest from looking at this, that there should be a third writer. Without full information, the society won't know how to process this (as we'll see in the registrations section further on).

Chapter 6: What Is The Length Of Copyright?

In the UK, the length of copyright in publishing rights is currently set at 70 years after the death of the last contributor. So, if there are four composers/authors on a work, then the work will be in public domain (out of copyright) 70 years after the fourth writer dies.

The length of copyright used to be split between the top line melody and the lyrics. If the two elements were separated between writers, then the two halves would go out of copyright at different times (assuming the contributors died on different days). See the example below:

Writer	Role	IPI No.	Performance	Mechanical	Date of Death
Heidle, Luke	C	10101024	33.33%	33.33%	01/09/1930
Clarke, Lucy	A	20203048	33.33%	33.33%	08/10/1947

Here, the musical element was in public domain from 1 September 2000 but the lyrics wouldn't be in public domain until 8 October 2017.

As of 1 November 2013, due to a legislative change, these will no longer be considered as separate elements. For any work where either the lyrics or the melody are still in copyright but the other is now in public domain, this part will now be pulled back into the other's copyright term. For any work where both elements are out of copyright, then this term has truly passed and the work will remain in public domain status.

This only counts if both the melody and the lyrics were written with the intention of creating the one, whole work. For example, a poem that is due to enter public domain, cannot be extended just because someone makes it into a song. Reworking your grandfather's guitar riff from one of his old songs, into a rap number, will mean that the lyrics are in copyright until 70 years after your death but the music will still be considered as separate.

You may be wondering how discussing copyright length will help you if you don't have to worry about it until you've been dead for a long time and come back during a musical, zombie apocalypse. Well, it may be more useful in terms of using other people's material. If you wish to cover someone's copyrighted material then this is usually fine but you won't receive publishing royalties. If you wish to change someone's work and either receive a share in the new work or still leave the original writer(s) with all of the publishing credit, you will need to request their permission, which could be a lengthy and even disappointing process if rejected (we'll discuss this later).

A work that is in the public domain, however, is free for you to use (and abuse) as you please. There are two types of public domain contributions. DP (derived from the French, 'Domaine Public') or PD (Public Domain) refer to works which were in copyright but no longer are. In these works, the original writer(s) are identified and dates of copyright expiration are available. Traditional works, on the other hand, are works which have been passed along through many generations but their origins aren't known, precisely. A lot of folk musicians in the UK play traditional works at nearly every gig.

As soon as you create an arrangement of a work within the public domain, you become the arranger, a sole share holder in the new arrangement (or alongside any co-arrangers). If you read straight from someone else's sheet music or copy them exactly, then there may be grounds for someone to challenge your performance as that of their arrangement. But, largely, you'll be paid as though you were the writer of this work. Here are a couple of examples:

Marie's Wedding					
Writer	Role	IPI Number	Performance	Mechanical	Status
Trad	CA	473321567	0.00%	0.00%	DP
Clarke, Lucy	Arr	20203048	100.00%	100.00%	

5th Symphony					
Writer	Role	IPI Number	Performance	Mechanical	Status
Van Beethoven, Ludwig	C	75607366	0.00%	0.00%	DP
Clarke, Lucy	Arr	20203048	100.00%	100.00%	

This means that even someone who travels around the country, playing small gigs of purely traditional and DP covers (such as the musician I mentioned earlier, with the 250-300 gigs in a year) can get paid publishing royalties.

It's unbelievable to think that in actual fact, a large chunk of royalties every year, aren't paid out to musicians that are entitled to them. Either record labels keep them, works can't be identified, or most commonly, musicians aren't even aware that they are entitled to them and should be claiming.

This is probably the greatest inspiration behind this book. During my career, I have met hundreds of musicians who had no idea they were missing royalties. I have even met musicians who were fully aware of the collection societies but never got round to joining,or didn't realise there was one particular area where they had missed out on royalties.

Anything that PRS For Music collects, it attempts to distribute. If they cannot locate you or your work, it may be that the top-earning songwriters receive extra royalties. Ensure that you're collecting what is due to you.

7. So, What IS A Music Publisher?

7.1. Defining A Music Publisher

So far, we've discussed how you can use collection societies to help you keep on track of your music publishing royalties. So where does a music publisher comes into the picture?

A music publisher is a company that represents your publishing rights. There are two reasons for this. The first is that, so far, we've encountered what could be described as the 'less complicated' end of the spectrum. A music publisher specialises in this area and can deal with varying scenarios so that you don't have to. You could have passed this book by and given everything over to a music publisher to take care of on your behalf.

The second is that they can take on the remaining rights that the societies haven't. They can negotiate synch fees to your advantage and they can license out print products.

My suggestion for anyone serious (or even casual) about their music, is to do all of this yourself directly and with PRS For Music until you're either far too busy with licensing requests, adaptation requests and third parties releasing your products to do it yourself, or you are breaking through into international markets (which makes not having a publisher VERY tricky).

On top of this, if you're not bringing in a lot yet and don't have a record of writing for artists, and therefore you'll likely find it extremely tough to get a publishing deal in the first place. This book aims to ensure that you understand the sector and don't miss out on royalties until then.

7.2. Publishing Rates

Publishing rates differ, depending on how much work you'll need done, how successful you are (giving you leverage), how much risk is involved, whether you're getting an advance and what's included in the deal (such as rights, material and territories). They often go from between a few percent up to about 25% cut to the publisher.

7.3. Publishers And Synch Leverage

If an advertising agency want to use one of your songs then you may find a chunk of your income going to the publisher (e.g. 15-20%). But it could be that it was the publisher that secured the synch, by pitching your song to the advertising agency in the first place.

I once came across a situation, where a young band were offered a synch opportunity for a UK television advert for a top clothing brand. They were told that the agency only had a small budget for the musical element, even though music is extremely important on adverts, as most major brands are fully aware. The band were advised by multiple, uninvolved parties to hold their ground and push for more from the agency but the agency threatened to use a different track if they didn't accept. Worried that they would miss out on such a great promotional opportunity, they walked away with £200 and a pair of boots each. They didn't get as much promotion from the advert as they had hoped to and missed out on thousands of pounds.

A publisher usually has set rates for the use of a track and has more power to stick to those rates. They often have a good relationship with agencies, who want to maintain it.

7.4. A Breathing Space Between You And The Publishing Sector

A publisher will register all of your music for you with the societies, to ensure that there are no problems. If you provide details of products

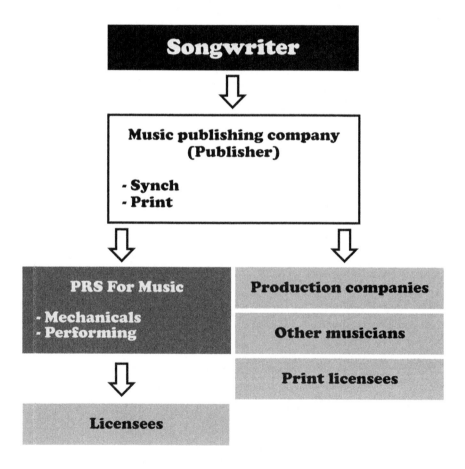

Figure 5.

released with your music to them, they will track those products and lean on the society and record label to get royalties to you.

In the same way that an artist manager's role is often described as a 'breathing space between the artist and the industry', a music publisher essentially represents a breathing space between the writer or their management, and the music-publishing sector. This is what makes the new structure of music publishing for the UK a bit more like the one presented above, in figure 5.

It is possible to negotiate directly with a music publisher in order to retain certain rights and deal with it yourself. However, doing something like that may affect the resulting rates or even the willingness of a publisher to sign a deal.

8. Different Publishing Deals

8.1. When Does A Publisher Come On Board?

A publisher usually comes on board later on in a musician's career. It's less usual for a publisher to actively promote their writers to the extent that a record label would (although it does happen).

The main focus of a publisher is to assist you in collecting royalties that are out there or will be out there, and to help with the licensing process. Please note and remember that music publishers are not there to make musicians famous. They could promote you in some small ways, such as through a press release or website material, but they won't plaster streets with posters.

The area where promotion does occur are synchs. The synch teams usually build relationships with advertising agencies, channel staff, production companies etc., in order to help their material to get used.

They may also help by putting on small gigs for press and potential licensees, or by inviting people to your gigs to hear your music, resulting in a possible synch opportunity.

8.2. Creative Deals

The above is a common publishing deal, whereby the publisher focuses on collecting, and makes up the vast majority of deals.

A different type of deal, and one that is far harder to come by, is a creative deal or songwriting deal. In this situation, the publisher sees a talent in you and you are willing to write for other artists. If you have a strong songwriting talent, then they may pick you up at an early stage. More likely, they'll look for material you have already written for others and how well it's been done, but on many an occasion within this category, the writer is inexperienced and mainly holds a talent.

The publisher will pitch your songs to artists nationally and/or internationally (depending on the deal territories), and see if they can get other artists to record and use your material, or co-write with you. The downside to this is that there may be limits on what you can use yourself, of your own material. Most songwriters in the UK, have the intention of performing those songs themselves as the artist.

In a deal like this, the word 'cover' is often thrown around. In this context, it means a work which has been successfully pitched to an artist by the publisher and therefore they are likely to receive a higher rate for it. Be careful of the two meanings for 'cover recording' used in the music industry.

8.3. Administration Deals Vs. Ownership Deals

When signing, it should be made clear what is happening to the actual copyrights of your material. In an administrative deal, the publisher will not own the rights to any of your works, but will hold the exclusive right to collect for you (and take their percentage share) for a set length of time. They cannot use a piece of music without your permission, such as in synchs.

If someone wants to change your music in any way, the publisher will require your permission first (assuming that you have not previously authorised them to agree to everything; some musicians do this if they don't want to have to think about anything other than playing and recording).

The upside to an administrative deal is that you retain all legal rights to a work and have considerably more control. The downside, however, is that the music publisher cannot offer legal advice or assistance if there are problems in this area. As the administrator, and not copyright owner, it isn't their responsibility, or often their legal right, to get involved.

On the flip side, an ownership deal, where a percentage of each work is actually owned by the publisher for the life of copyright, or for a set amount of time, leaves the writer with far less control. As an owner in the work, the publisher does not require the writer's permission to allow adaptations of their work, synch usage or give room for moral exclusions (such as if a burger chain wanted to use a piece of music by a strict vegetarian), although sometimes the writer insists on including moral exclusions in the deal.

On a positive note, the publisher will invest its own money into legally protecting your work. Also, if you're well known or build a good relationship with them (or simply to maintian good practice), they'll often ask for your approval on synchs and adaptations out of courtesy.

Keep in mind that if you sign up to a long-term deal, at some point in the future, they may decide to sell their share in your work or particular catalogues. They may get bought up by a rival company or merge. This could leave you with a less preferable company, or leave your works scattered between various different entities. If you signed with a company because you had built up a good relationship with one of their A&R/Sales team, that person could be long gone by the time your deal expires (if it ever does, and isn't for the life of copyright).

It's worth keeping this in mind when negotiating the length of a deal. If you aren't as bothered about retaining your copyrights and don't feel their worth will grow more than the publisher predicts, then many musicians are happy to sell a part in their works or give away ownership in exchange for a large advance.

If a publisher wants to buy out a work entirely, then they are able to, for a one-off payment. Or they could commission you to write the piece. These publishers are usually categorised as 'library publishers'.

8.4. What Is A Library Publisher?

A library publisher often accumulates many different kinds of works in their entirety, and divides them into genre, mood, instrumentation, speed, etc. An agency or licensee that is looking for a type of music and wants to avoid the inconvenience of going to lots of different writers or publishers to obtain the license, can go to a library publisher and avoid much of the hassle. They won't be able to find commercial charting works here, though.

8.5. Work For Hire

This is different from a library work, although ownership of the work is given to the production company. The company could pay you a one-off fee or wage in order to write a piece or ongoing pieces of music for them. Anything that you write for them will also be owned by them. They could ask you to write a fun, childish song for a new line of plastic toys that they are bringing out, for example, or a synch piece to become the theme song for a new sci-fi series in production.

These agreements can change from one to the another. In some situations, the production company owns everything to do with the work and collects all of the resulting royalties (usually the production company will have a publishing arm, such as Disney, or they will assign all of the works to an external publisher to look after). For instance, he BBC pays musicians to create their own sound effects. In other situations, they only agree that they won't have to pay a synch fee, but the writer will still receive any performance income from broadcasts or mechanical income from DVD and soundtrack sales.

8.6. Co-Publishing Deals

When involved in music publishing, you will no doubt continuously hear the terms 'writer's share' and 'publisher's share'. It comes from the olden days, when many artists did not write their own material but relied on others to write it for them. It was one of the main jobs of a publisher to pitch your work to other writers and performing artists. As such, the whole process of writing the original material, pitching to artists and collecting/distributing royalties, was seen as a team effort and the songwriter's share in a work was split down the middle, 50/50 with the publisher.

Fifty percent of the songwriter's share was referred to as the 'writer's share' and the other half of the songwriter's share was referred to as the 'publisher's share'.

Moving into modern times, most writers of music have the intention of performing the work themselves and so the publisher's jobs has been somewhat reduced. Shares are rarely split 50/50 unless there is a big advance or the publisher has purchased half of the work.

The two halves are still referred to as the publisher's share and the writer's share. The writer's performing share, 50%, is paid directly to the writer by PRS For Music, as mentioned earlier.

A co-publishing deal is where a writer wishes to retain more control in a work, and so creates a publishing entity for half of the publisher's share (25% of their whole share) and assigns or sells the other half (25% of their whole share) to another publisher. This, in theory, increases their control, synch opportunities (two companies pitching) and efficiency (two companies tracking royalties). Often, the writer assigns their co-publishing share to a second publisher to administer, offering all of the above but with little effort from the writer. Nevertheless, it is likely that publishers will be discouraged if you aren't generating lots of income. It could also mean that production companies are put off by having to speak to two companies to clear your interest in a work.

8.7. Agreement Lengths

An agreement length is important, as you need to be able to get out of a deal if you don't feel that the publisher is doing a good job. A common administrative deal length for a well-known writer is about 2-3 years, which gives the publisher enough time to get up and running, while being short enough for the writer to pull out if the deal isn't working.

The bigger the risk, or the greater the advance that you receive, the longer is the term likely to be. The publisher wants to be sure that if you have taken an advance of £30 000, they will be able to recoup the investment, at the very least. Ideally they will also be able to generate profit on top of that. The point is, as in any busines, to not lose money.

At the end of the set time-frame, there is usually the preferred option of a 'rolling period'. This is where the deal goes on indefinitely, until either the writer or the publisher decides to terminate the deal. The writer may decide to go elsewhere or the publisher may find the writer difficult to deal with, for very little in return. Usually the contract will state a notice period, such as 3 months.

Once the rights period has ended (the set term and any rolling period, where rights are owned or administered by the publisher), there is usually a collection period. Because royalties take so long to flow, it can take a while for them to get back to the publisher and writer, especially when talking about foreign territories.

Usually a collection period of 1-2 years is common. During this time-frame, the writer can sign to another publisher, but the first publisher is entitled to any royalties that come through from usage of when the deal was active. If a payment comes into the society, say three years late and the collection period is over, then the new publisher is entitled to these royalties, even though they were from when the writer was in their old deal. It's more like a set time-frame for the old publisher to 'grab what's theirs or lose it'.

If an advance has been given, then there may be a clause in the contract to say that the deal cannot end until the advance has been recouped. There is often also a clause in this situation, allowing the writer to end the deal if they pay back the unrecouped balance, plus a charge (e.g pay back 120% of unrecouped balance).

If a share in the works is purchased, then the period of the purchased section will be for 'life of copyright', as they now own these shares.

8.8. Advances

Many musicians dream of an advance, which could buy them a car, a house and a guitar-shaped swimming pool. Bear in mind that publishers don't like too much risk and will likely only give you what they feel you're likely to recoup sometime soon.

While you are in an 'unrecouped state' (you owe the publisher money and haven't recouped your advance) the rates are usually weighted a bit more in favour of the publisher. The publisher therefore receives a greater percentage of what comes in, and the rest is used to recoup the advance.

It may be that you plan to use the advance to invest in a tour, a new album, equipment or promotion, in which case it could be better to take it. It's worth trying to avoid, however, taking an advance of a couple of thousand pounds unless you really need it, as you may be better off without it. Even once recouped, the contract will likely include a clause to say that the publisher's increased percentage will be in place for a couple of months afterwords. This is usually for accounting purposes and nothing vicious, but it's worth weighing up when deciding whether or not to take an advance.

8.9. The Universe

You may encounter, outside of the normal territories, a reference to somewhere along the lines of 'the Earth, the universe and everywhere within it'. When airplanes started to play music and locations such as the international space station, orbiting the Earth, there was a bit of confusion over who actually controlled the rights. Now, just to be sure, everywhere is contained in the contract. So when we finally colonize the moon and Mars, your faithful publisher and other licensing parties will be on hand to mould a new revenue stream.

Chapter 9: The UK Registration Process

9.1. The Publisher Pathway

So far, we've looked into understanding UK music publishing but I want to touch on some areas on an international level too. One of the main reasons for this is to show how valuable a publishing deal can be when you start breaking into foreign markets. Another is to show just how complicated the registration process can be.

The registration process refers to the procedure of letting the various entities know of a work's existence, how it is split up between writers and who represents each writer (as each writer could have a deal with a different publisher) in terms of the mechanical and performing rights.

First, have a look at figure 6 showing how this would work in the UK. Then compare to figure 7, showing what happens if there is more than one writer on a work. If they are both represented by the same publisher, then there isn't much of a difference. If each writer has signed with a different publisher, however, the structure will look like the one shown in figure 8.

Figure 6.

Figure 7.

Figure 8.

9.2. Multiple Registrations

If two co-writers register for their share in a work, PRS For Music are left with two registrations. One from Writer A and the other from Writer B. These two registrations need to be merged. This is where the point made earlier, about the complete work splits being required, comes into play. Can you imagine if the society were left with the two registrations below?

I Love To Sing				
Writer	**Role**	**IPI Number**	**Performance**	**Mechanical**
Heidle, Luke	CA	10101024	50.00%	50.00%

I Love To Sing				
Writer	**Role**	**IPI Number**	**Performance**	**Mechanical**
Clarke, Lucy	CA	20203048	50.00%	50.00%

With uncommon names, for example if the work were called 'Hexagon 2198736', then it would be easy to match up two work registrations. Something as common as the title of the above work, however, would leave little evidence that these were two parts of the same work. Now you can see why complete information is required. When two incoming registrations are the same, work registrations can be merged together to form a complete entry on the database:

I Love To Sing				
Writer	**Role**	**IPI Number**	**Performance**	**Mechanical**
Heidle, Luke	CA	10101024	50.00%	50.00%
Clarke, Lucy	CA	20203048	50.00%	50.00%

9.3. Automated Matching

To save time and manual workload, in merging every related registration received into single works, when so many are inactive and not receiving royalties (quite a lot, permanently) an auto-matching system is in place. Where the system recognises two works with a similar title and writers then it creates a match. When one of the work registrations is linked to usage and due to be paid out on, a member of staff manually checks the matches and merges the two (or more) entries together. If a second registration has been sent in afterwords, with a correction, then at this point the work will be manually updated as per the most recent registration.

9.4. Why Should I Register If Someone Else Already Has?

So why does more than one writer or publisher have to supply the society with the same information? There are two reasons for this. The first is that the writer and/or their representing publisher, who registers their share on the work, cannot have their share removed afterwords, without first giving permission to the society and being made aware.

Another writer, who hasn't registered for their share, can be removed at any time, or have some of their shares removed without being told, if a different writer tells the society that they contributed to the work (whether falsely or not). Therefore it's best for each party to register for their claim. It's also a good idea to agree work splits with your co-writers (preferably in a letter signed by all parties) to avoid future disagreements and to provide evidence of your claim.

The second reason is that some societies do not allow one writer, or their publisher, to allocate shares to another party. This is the case with MCPS. Remember that PRS For Music is a combination of two previously merged companies, MCPS and PRS. PRS allow the allocation of shares to others but MCPS do not. MCPS require each writer, or their representing publisher, to register for their own share. Until they do so, the unregistered mechanical shares are placed into an account called 'Copyright Control'.

Here is an example of a work, where Luke Heidle has registered for his 50% share but Lucy Clarke has not yet got round to it:

I Love To Sing				
Writer	**Role**	**IPI Number**	**Performance**	**Mechanical**
Heidle, Luke	CA	10101024	50.00%	50.00%
Clarke, Lucy	CA	20203048	50.00%	
Copyright Control				50.00%

Thanks to Luke's registration, Lucy will receive performing royalties for radio, television, live performance etc. but will miss out on digital royalties permanently unless she registers. No record labels will be invoiced for her mechanical share either, unless she registers for mechanicals. Another party could come in and take her performing share, as she has not officially registered for it. If Luke wasn't sure what Lucy's IPI number was, then the work wouldn't be linked to her account and she wouldn't receive anything:

I Love To Sing				
Writer	Role	IPI Number	Performance	Mechanical
Heidle, Luke	CA	10101024	50.00%	50.00%
Clarke, Lucy	CA	?	50.00%	
Copyright Control				50.00%

The bottom line therefore is to always remember that if you don't have a publisher, you have to make sure to proactively register all of your works with the society.

9.5. How Does Publisher's Registration Differ From Writer's?

When a writer is published, the royalties flow through the publisher, who will pay the writer's shares directly minus their agreed commission. The work will then look something like this (Chain of Title represents a link between a writer(s) and a publishing entity to show which writer(s) that publisher represents):

I Love To Sing					
Writer	Role	Chain of Title	IPI Number	Performance	Mechanical
Heidle, Luke	CA	A	10101024	25.00%	
Clarke, Lucy	CA		20203048	50.00%	50.00%
Music Rocks Publishing Ltd	Publisher	A	74639273	25.00%	50.00%

This shows that Music Rocks Publishing Ltd, is the publisher for Luke Heidle, and that Lucy Clarke isn't published and has registered for her share as well (because she has her mechanical share assigned to her, otherwise it would be in Copyright Control).

9.6. Writer's Performing Share

Something that you may have noticed is the fact that half of Luke's performance share is still allocated to his account, rather than it all being allocated to Music Rocks Publishing Ltd. This is because the writer gets paid half of the performing share directly in the UK. The 50% of the songwriter's performing share cannot be removed from them and must be paid directly to the writer.

The exception to this rule is where a writer isn't a member of PRS For Music (or a foreign collection society) or their membership number cannot be identified (the publisher hasn't told to society what it is), then the 50% performance share is passed onto the publisher, to pay through to the writer in good faith. Note that this will then be subjected to the publisher's commission rate. Some less reputable publishers deliberately prevent the collection society from identifying the exact account, so that they can receive 100% of the writer's share and commission the extra. Most publishers, however, will happily accept your IPI number. It is therefore worth ensuring that they are aware of it so that they can include it on their works registrations.

9.7. Is It Always 50% Of The Writer's Performing Share?

In the United States, the 50% performing rule is the same but other territories differ. For example, with the collection society STIM in Sweden, the writer often retains 66.67% of their performing share. This book concentrates mostly on the UK sector but please keep in mind that once you move into foreign territories, the rules change.
As previously mentioned, having a publisher at this point is invaluable.

9.8. The Duplicate Claims Process

What happens if registrations differ? To get an idea, have a look at what happens in the two tables opposite:

I Love To Sing				
Writer	**Role**	**IPI Number**	**Performance**	**Mechanical**
Heidle, Luke	CA	10101024	50.00%	50.00%
Clarke, Lucy	CA	20203048	50.00%	50.00%

I Love To Sing				
Writer	**Role**	**IPI Number**	**Performance**	**Mechanical**
Heidle, Luke	CA	10101024	66.66%	66.66%
Clarke, Lucy	CA	20203048	33.34%	33.34%

When this happens, it's known as a 'possible duplicate claim'. The first claimant is the party that sent in the registration first and the second claimant is the party that sent in their registration second. In a possible duplicate claim, one or both of the parties will be contacted to clarify if this was a mistake or if they both maintain the claim that they have registered. Where one was a mistake, the registration will either be amended or the faulting party will be required to re-register the work.

In situations where both parties confirm that there has not been a mistake in their registered splits, the work will be escalated to 'duplicate claim' status. The second claimant will be given a time period (usually 60-90 days) to back up their claim. If they cannot do so, then the work will be updated in favour of the first claimant. If the second claimant can back up their claim, then the first claimant will be given a time period to produce evidence. If both parties can prove their claim, then the work is escalated further to a 'dispute' status. In dispute, no royalties are paid out until the dispute has been resolved, often through the courts. PRS For Music don't get involved in this process. This is also the point where publishers in a purely administrative deal will leave you to 'sort it out amongst yourselves'.

Often, what is used to back up a claim, is either a contract between writers, signed by all contributing parties, agreeing on the share split for the work or a signed statement from the writer to say that their shares are correct. The first is more straightforward and is hard to dispute but the second is merely a legal statement, that can cause a lot of problems if no further evidence can be produced.

The bottom line is to ensure that you register promptly to hold the upper hand as first claimant and, more importantly, to ensure that any share agreements between co-writers are put to paper and signed. Although you may be writing with close friends now, there's no telling what will happen further down the line. If one of your songs becomes a hit and there's nothing on paper, it can cause a lot more hassle than if you had just planned ahead and made a registration in time.

9.9. What To Keep In Mind When Agreeing Splits

When agreeing splits for your works, it's all too easy to just split equally amongst the band. This is fine if everyone contributes to the writing of a work equally but if they don't then it's worth considering if they should even be receiving a share.

It's not uncommon for one member to leave the band but continue to hold a share in a work. With that share they have the ability to deny synchs and will get paid every time you play the song live. On rare occasions, introducing a new member to the group results in the group deciding to give the new person a share (diluting those of the remaining writers). This would be an act of good will and not recommended, usually only where the band feel that the new person has brought something to the song. In the below example, if writer 5 leaves, the rest are left with a lower share, even though they're the ones actively promoting the song:

Writer	Role	Performance	Mechanical
Writer 1	CA	20.00%	20.00%
Writer 2	CA	20.00%	20.00%
Writer 3	CA	20.00%	20.00%
Writer 4	CA	20.00%	20.00%
Writer 5	**CA**	**20.00%**	**20.00%**

Writer	Role	Performance	Mechanical
Writer 1	CA	16.00%	16.00%
Writer 2	CA	16.00%	16.00%
Writer 3	CA	16.00%	16.00%
Writer 4	CA	16.00%	16.00%
Writer 5	**CA**	**20.00%**	**20.00%**
Writer 6 (new)	**CA**	**16.00%**	**16.00%**

If you are the main songwriter of a group, then consider creating an agreement with the group (and getting them to sign it) saying that you retain, or stay close to, 100% of the stated works but you will divide the royalties equally, so long as they are still in the group.

10. The Worldwide Registration Process

10.1. Registering In Multiple Territories

The previous sections presented a summary of how collection societies split out royalties received for music usage. This is simple when just dealing with PRS For Music in the UK but take a look at figure 9 representing a chart of how a publisher deals with collection societies over a few example territories. As you can see, it's the same line of relationships from writer to licensee in each territory.

10.2. Original Publishers And Sub Publishers

When a writer's material really starts to take off internationally, it can become harder to keep track of what's going on, especially if a publisher is looking after hundreds, thousands or even millions of works.

An original publisher, is the publishing company that a writer signs a deal with, usually within their home territory, or the territory where their music first 'took off'.

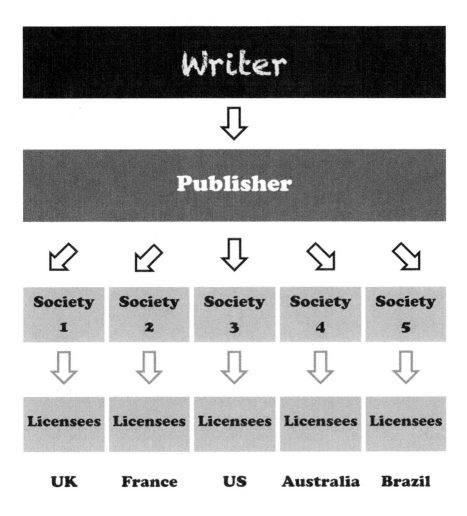

Figure 9.

A sub-publisher is an entity that the original publisher uses to look after its works in a different territory. The sub-publisher is more familiar with their territory, speaks the language, is based there for meetings and synch pitching opportunities and usually holds a relationship and membership with their local society. A graph of the original publisher to sub-publisher relationship is shown in figure 10.

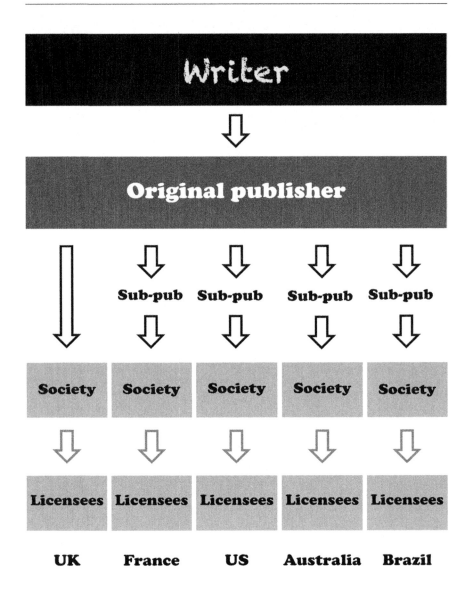

Figure 10.

A sub-publisher can just be a different office, within the same company as the original publisher (figure 11). Sub-publishers will take a cut of your earnings as well but all of this information is available in your contract and while negotiating. If you agree to pay your original pub-

Figure 11.

lisher 20% of your worldwide earnings, then they will likely be getting all 20% of their home territory, and splitting this with the sub-publishers in the other territories, for everything that comes through them.

11. Be Careful Out There

11.1. Synch Opportunities

It is easy to be drawn in by the opportunity of getting your music in a movie, advert or TV show but think carefully before committing to anything. Product advertising is a fierce industry and advertisers will not want to use a song to back their product when a competitor, or an unrelated product, can use the same track. They want consumers to think of their brand when hearing your songs and will likely be keen on using your work exclusively for a set period of time. This could mean that you miss out on a different opportunity, which could have also paid more money.

Once your work becomes linked to a product then most other companies will not want to touch it. One example is the use of The Rembrandts' *I'll Be There For You* on the hit TV series *Friends*. This was obviously a great choice as *Friends* is still aired daily around the world and they're getting paid constantly but if the show had been a disaster, then they would not have found other TV show calling. The song will forever be '*Friends*' theme'.

11.2. 360 Degree Models

Something that is seeing an explosion is a set up referred to as the '360 degree model'. As some areas of the music industry are declining in revenues, such as record labels, they are seeking to increase their profit margins. Other startup companies want to get more involved in their act and there are often very good intentions behind a lot of these.

In a 360 degree model, an entity or a person looks after many different aspects of your musical career. This could be a mix of management, label services, publishing, PR, touring, production, promotion, merchandise, and anything else.

There are two things to watch out for in this model. The first one is saying that the music industry is straightforward and easy to understand. That is an outright lie. Each area is filled with people who have spent their lives learning from mistakes and experiences. To assume that someone can have an in-depth knowledge of several different areas sends a warning shot through the air. If it is a company that has employed different people from different areas, in order to provide a great service, then great. If it's your uncle Mark then think twice.

The second is that a conflict of interest is present. A single company would likely mean that you are receiving a higher percentage, as all areas can be streamlined, rather than many companies taking a cut of your profits. Be careful though or you may find that the pool of money you're getting your cut from is smaller than if a separate company was involved.

For example, many small record labels offer publishing deals to their artists. Apart from having little experience in this area, their main intention is to prevent another publishing company from ensuring MCPS invoices them for the release of the writer's material. They won't be as specialised at tracking or collecting your income and you won't get any publishing income from the products they're releasing. But hey, here's an extra couple of percent of anything that happens to land at their door.

Another example is where your manager has his own label or a publishing company. Of course they would rather sign you to them than have you get a better deal elsewhere.

11.3. Be wary of advances

If you ask an aspiring musician what their dream is then the answer often is – alongside stories Led Zeppelin would have been proud of – the offer of a large advance.

As managers, lawyers and accountants often work on a percentage commission of your income, some will push for a large advance as it will mean a lot of money going to them for doing not a lot of work. They will also be fully aware that by the time you start making significant money, you may have replaced them and so why not cash in now? Moreover, you have to factor in taxes surrounding large payments.

In order to get a large cash payment, there are always negatives. Either part of your copyrights are being sold or you are receiving less favourable rates until recouped. For example, if you're entering a deal with an 80/20 split between you and your publisher then it could be that the split during recoupment is 70/30, 60/40 or 50/50. So it will take longer to recoup with the publisher receiving a higher profit margin for the same amount of work. The contract will also state that once you recoup, the less favourable rates will be in place until the end of their specified accounting period. Although this is for accounting purposes, not to get one over on you, it will still happen.

The publisher is, of course, taking a risk by offering you an advance and, as it is with any loan, they're getting something out of it. In a scenario where you feel as if you will never make as much as the advance is, for example, when you plan to retire but haven't told the publisher so and they think that you're going to write more hits, then it could be best to cash in. To avoid this happening, many publishers give advances following the release of an album or when sales hit a certain level. If you're a global superstar and recoupment is not a gamble, and you can guarantee that you'll be bringing in a lot of money for the publisher, then you'll naturally be able to easily negotiate great rates. In that case you'd be able to enjoy the ideal – big advance and no change in rates before and after recoupment.

11.4. Industry Norms

With anything discussed in this book, many of the sections merely describe industry norms and aren't set in stone. I constantly come across unique deals, where the publisher wants to sign a writer or company and is willing to go out of their way for them.

There are step advances, which are given after the writer has earned certain amounts of royalties, different escalation dates that come into play in different situations, different reporting methods just for the individual writer and terms whereby different parts rights or works into or out of deals.

Splits don't have to be as simple as 80/20 or 50/50 etc, they can be as complicated as each right (synch, performing, mechanical, print) all having different splits between the writer and publisher. Certain territories can be included or excluded as of certain dates, different territories could hold different rates (e.g. mechanicals are 80/20 in UK but 75/25 for the rest of Europe). Unless bound by law, you are free to use your imagination. Just be careful that the more complex the deal, the harder it could be for you or the publisher to monitor and account correctly and could also discourage the publisher from working with you, if you are going to be too much hassle. Some well known writers try to include ridiculous clauses in their deals, just to see what they can get away with, as a kind of ego boost.

11.5. Publishing In The United States

Every territory has its own rules, depending on what the laws and regulations are. The US is different in many ways. For instance, publishers don't have to go through a collection society like MCPS to license product releases (although they can choose to go through Harry Fox for a fee) and they can license them directly.

It has been exlained earlier that MCPS have a set fee that they charge the record label, depending on which scheme they fall under. In the US, however, there are different rules and record labels hold more power. A set fee exists of around 9.1 cents per track (called the 'statutory rate') per copy distributed for tracks under 5 minutes and this changes for songs longer than above 5 minutes. There are maximum song allowances and the rate can be reduced under certain circumstances (e.g. advancing money to the publisher).

Labels often include a controlled composition clause when they sign an artist. This means that for any songs that the artist has written themselves, they (and subsequently their publisher) will receive a reduced rate. Some publisher are entering into direct deals with digital service providers in the US, such as Youtube, rather than going through the performance societies.

There are three performance societies like PRS For Music in the UK, namely ASCAP, BMI and SESAC. SESAC is a privately owned company, ASCAP was set up by publishers and BMI was set up by the broadcasting music industry. They have different ways of collecting and distributing royalties and you will need to choose one if your music is used over there, to license out your works to licensees.

Hopefully from the brief paragraphs above, you can see just how much things change between territories and as such should prove a good reason to enter into agreements with publishers who know their territory well and can look after your works. Remember that this book is aimed towards UK musicians and songwriters.

11.6. Illegal Downloading

As soon as someone even says the words 'illegal download', it is often met by two conflicting reactions. People are either sternly against it or they don't see a problem with it at all and have over four years worth of music spilling out of their hard-drives.

There have been situations over the past few years, where people who have downloaded music illegally have been made an example of. The reason behind it being that musicians have created a piece of work through sweat and tears, only to have it stolen from them.

Note that often it is the record label deciding to take legal action.

Largely, the only form of income that they receive is from the sale of the product or track download. If this is taken for free, then the record label receives nothing.

Many artists are actually in favour of giving their music away for free, a recent example being Radiohead, who decided to offer their album either for free or for a donation, decided by the fan.

The more people listen to your recordings, the more people will, in theory, attend your live shows, purchase your merchandise and spread your name. The money gained from other sources of income, such as streaming and live performance, can often make up for the amount lost through illegal downloads, so it is up to you how you feel about this.

It is doubtful that you will find a publisher who is open about this, however, as no matter how balanced the income becomes, it still makes the statement that the song download is worth nothing. Nobody who is passionate about the music they write or the music that they represent, will be comfortable with the message that their material is worthless.

11.7. Pan-European Licensing and Central European Licensing

Sometimes it's not even as simple as MCPS licensing and collecting for any mechanical income in the UK. As the world has been brought closer together by the internet and improved telecommunications and transport, the music industry has also been changing.

Pan-European licensing is where a website or online service pays one society for a license that covers the whole of Europe. The large publishers decide which society to invest their digital rights in and online services must then obtain a license from that society. This is fairly new and makes the process easier for both the online company and for the publisher, as neither side has to deal with multiple societies in multiple territories.

Central European Licensing is similar to this but refers to licenses for physical products. A major record label that covers Europe will likely choose a society to pay one license fee to, and obtain a license for the whole of Europe.

It is unlikely that you will be striking a deal of this nature (unless the industry continues to evolve in this direction) but you may find that your publisher has. This will affect you in a few ways. The time taken for royalties to reach you can be increased or decreased, the amount that you receive (without multiple societies 'skimming the cream') could rise and reporting levels could be more precise. On the other hand, reporting levels might also reflect which countries your royalties were being generated in with less accuracy. You may just see a lot of royalties coming from GEMA (the collection society in Germany) for this one license, for example.

You may also find societies trying to outbid each other in order to issue Central European licenses to a record label. As the bids get lower and lower, the number of royalties that you receive will get lower and lower, also.

11.8. Global Domination

You don't have to use one collection society to look after your works, you just cannot have more than one collecting for you in the same territory.

If you join PRS For Music in the UK, the common set up will be that they collect on your behalf for the world. You will need to let them know of international activity and it will take a lot longer to reach you, but they can collect on your behalf.

Performing rights societies have a close network and you will find that they are more accurate and likely to receive your royalties than mechanical rights societies. If you don't have a publisher, then it's always best to join the mechanical rights society in each territory that you have physical releases in.

If you wish, you could join multiple societies for different territories, which would mean faster payments, more accurate monitoring of what's going on and possible tax benefits. For example, you could join PRS For Music in the UK, GEMA in Germany for Europe excluding the UK, ASCAP and Harry Fox for the US and Canada, APRA-AMCOS in Australia for Australasia, ABRAMUS in Brazil for South America, etc. The amount of admin work, a few language barriers and inevitable misunderstandings of different rules and regulations for different territories, would mean that you would likely be better off getting yourself a publishing deal. If you are at this level of international success, then part with some of your income to bring in the experts and you will likely even find that they pay for themselves from what would have been missed in terms of identifying revenue streams.

11.9. The Wild Wild East

As we have gone through the various structures and affiliations between collection societies and publisher in different territories, it's very much worth keeping in mind that some countries have less stable law enforcement when it comes to copyright.

Places such as India, China, some parts of South America, Africa and Russia (to name a few) have more pressing issues on their plates. China, for example, is currently dealing with massive growth, a move into an expanding middle class and accusations of human rights abuse, as well as a move into space and leading a cyber war. They have little time to worry about songwriters being paid by someone in another part of the country.

A few times I have had to explain this to writers who want to know why more isn't being done to get their money from these countries, where their music is clearly being used. If the government aren't reinforcing copyright law, then all you have to rely on is the good will of the person or company using the music to pay you. If they don't want to pay, then there isn't much that can be done.

One country, which will remain unnamed, claims to be active in its copyright protection and the society that collects on behalf of its writers, does license for music use but then not a lot comes out of the other end. The licensee can prove that a payment was made but the collection society insists that no payment was received. It prefers to pay writers from within its own territory but a fraction of international royalties are actually paid out.

11.10. Translations And Adaptations

If you find someone requesting to adapt or translate your work then take care to ensure that you are covered legally. Make certain to get a copy of the lyrics in English (unless you speak the language) and make sure that you are happy with it. If the new lyrics are offensive then you may not want to be linked to the new work.

If the other party has asked for a share, then see to it that they have changed it enough to warrant one. Is it still your input that drives the new song?

Most importantly, ensure that you are not held legally accountable. If they use an unauthorised sample of somebody else's work in their new song or break the law in any way, then you don't want to be associated with that. Get them to sign a brief statement, approving the adaptation under an agreement that they will be held responsible for any such situation and that any additional share splits would be taken out of their part.

Usually, if someone is going to the effort of asking your permission in the first place though, it is doubtful that they would be out to cause harm and use someone else's contribution without permission.

11.11. Who Else Can Get A Share In Your Work?

Do you have to be a writer on a work to gain a writing credit and share? The answer to this is no. It is not unusual for producers who have directed or mixed your recording to get a share. It is also not unusual for the artist, who is going to perform the song but has had no creative input in its making, to get a share.

It all depends on what they're bringing to the table. If it's a big artist or producer putting their name to it, if the person mixing the track has put a lot of effort into it and has given it a unique sound, or even if your manager is going to make you huge and decided to creatively force his way into your work by adding a single tambourine shake into the background at one point, you may decide to give a portion away.

Be extremely careful though. If someone is helping you out and you give away partial creative ownership, then they will have a right to it for the life of copyright and will have a say on whether synchs are approved, other use of the track or if it can be changed.

Also, don't leap into bed with the idea of your work being used by a major artist as it could work against your favour. Other than possibly giving a share in the work away, it will likely be contracted as an exclusive work for a certain time period, meaning that no other artist can release the work for a while. If possible, find out whether it will make the album or better yet, be released as a single. It's arguably better to have your song released as a single by a band of medium fame, than as a forgotten B-side by a larger artist.

Conclusion

With over a decade of experience in the music publishing industry, I have worked with many top artists and songwriters from around the world. Helping to administer the catalogues and collect royalties across the globe of a wide variety of acts, from rock legends such as The Beatles, Sonic Youth and The Clash to more modern acts such as Thom Yorke and One Direction. Stage writers like George and Ira Gershwin, jazz and funk artists like Herbie Hancock and George Clinton to Folkmusicians including The Battlefield Band.

Remember that this book is intended as a starting point for musicians and songwriters based in the UK and is not an extensive guide. If you wish to know more about music publishing in the UK then PRS For Music is an excellent place to start. As the industry is constantly evolving due to new technologies and laws, some areas of this book may be outdated in the not-too-distant future so it's always worth double-checking with an expert. Lastly, there are few rules in the music industry, only norms, so always do your best to ensure that you aren't being taken advantage of. Seek advice before you sign anything. Best of luck to you and your career – well done for being more creative than I am. There would be no industry without the music on which it runs.

Printed in Great Britain
by Amazon